The Live Science
of
Mathematics

*

essay

*

Traumear

*

These live sciences, like the present one, are works of transition from development to evolution. When a human being evolves he has to cope somehow with the fact that 'everything changes', even the meaning of 'everything' and of 'change'. How he goes about this, necessarily with the help of the spirit of truth, depends on his constitution and on his gifts or talents – in other words on what he brought with him into the world at his birth. Of course he must discover – and it will partly be revealed to him – how he is to work and what kind of work he is to do during his evolution. He is to die to the old world and to build up his endless world. Works which arise from such initial evolutionary impulses, such these live sciences like the present, will then stimulate and facilitate the transition in some others who are ready to evolve.

*

The Live Science of Mathematics

This is the science which relates number to name.

Number is a concept. A particular number is not a concept, but a name.

To name something means to identify it. Whatever has a name is useful. The appropriate name for a thing is that which limits it for total use.

Limitation by name is a category. The category which most successfully defines a thing allows it to unfold itself most freely. The category which defines a thing without allowing it to unfold itself is said to be blind. All blind categories are useless. An example of a blind category is the definition of substance as a thing which must be formed. Substance defined as the thing which shapes and transforms itself on the other hand is the definition of substance which is categorically sound. Consequently substance is a name.

That number which applies to a set of things renders those things adaptable. Adaptation is the single purpose of counting. When something has been counted it is not any more strange. The very purpose of counting is to bring things within the scope of our mastery. Those things which are mastered are mathematically clear. Categorical soundness and mathematical clarity reveal the relation. The relation has no other purpose. It is the final purpose. To treat a relation as a means towards an end means to disturb it essentially. An example of an essentially disturbed relation is equality as proof. When two things are equal this proves absolutely nothing, but it dos mean that they have been found to exist at the same time. It does no exclude the possibility of their existing at different times, in which case they could not be equal. Equality however as an achieved basis, not as a basis for this or that but as an independent basis, is an example of true relation, undisturbed and precise.

*

1

The mode of mathematical operation is the sign. In order to understand what a sign is it must be in operation. The significant operation is exact.

A sign may be either perfect or usual. The perfect sign implies the reason of the operation. The usual sign suggests the reason for the operation. In either case it is the sign which the operation relies upon, and the operation does not influence the sign.

An example of a sign is a graph. The graph shows what the case is. The operation arising from the graph is said to be casual. The perfect graph shows in what case a given situation happens to be. The situation in that case is numerically expressed and nominally demonstrated. The usual graph gives evidence of a given process in order. The process in that order is numerically impressed and nominally demonstrated. This was an example of a sign, of a perfect sign, and of a usual sign.

All signs originate. The origin of the sign illuminates it. This illumination makes the sign implicit or suggestive. The implicit sign reveals its origin. The suggestive sign discovers it. An example of an implicit sign revealing its origin is the letter p in the word pot when that word is heard but not understood. Contemplation of the letter p in that case brings it into focus as an alphabetical increment which carries meaning and which evokes a sensation, but for the meaning and the sensation to be joined, a third factor must be elicited, which due to an impingement upon the imagination allows the reception of particular sense data to egress as a limiting function, and this factor is the origin of the implicit sign, which in the case of our present example is a vessel for the sake of containing things. An example of a suggestive sign discovering its origin is the image of a tree which hovers before our eyes at this moment. We question the description of this tree and it may turn out to resemble an elder. We reproduce it as a drawing and perhaps observe it objectively for the sake of stylistic measurement. It creates in us its

2

subject which we either project into the drawing or superimpose upon it, or else we allow it to become one with that object so that the whole thing exists. Our drawing in any of these three cases represents the origin of the image with which we started, and that origin is the imagination, discovered by the suggestive sign which was the image of a tree.

The mathematical process is called an equation. Equations are either true or extant. The true equation is comprehended and not perceived, while the extant equation is perceived and not comprehended. An example of an extant equation is the human likeness of man and god. An example of a true equation is the name of the number six. The true equation in this latter example is comprehended as the problem which separates four from ten. The decimal system offers the context of this problem. In this system, and as an application of it, the number six is limited for the purpose of even division and it is adaptable in terms of the number of times in which it reproduces the number one. Division and reproduction make up the essence of multiplication. The number six has that particular name because it illustrates that essence completely. The illustration of an essence allows that essence to behave. Multiplication behaves in terms of a product and on the basis of a factor. In the case of the number six for instance, multiplication behaves in terms of two and three and on the basis of six and one. The numbers four and five, which do not entail multiplication in this instance, may be presumed to be subordinate factors, which support the mathematical process in question, because they do not rely upon each other. This reliance of numbers upon each other may be explained as an elementary relation. Elementary relations contain other relations. They may contain any possible relation or relations, even other elementary relations or simply another elementary relation. Their content is their definition. In the case of the numbers four and five for instance a lack of mutual reliance is the elementary relation which contains the number nine, not

3

because that is their sum, which it also happens to be, but merely so. The elementary relation which contains the number nine is defined by that number, not however by the number nine as a number, but as a relation. It so happens that the number nine is an elementary relation which contains and is defined by the relation of three to itself, which it called subjective relation and which in the case of the number three manifests itself perfectly. The manifestation of a relation makes it plain. Once a relation is plain it cannot be any further simplified and must be accepted if it is to become profitable. If attempts are made further to simplify a plain relation, then that relation is distorted, and it will seem to lead to other things which in fact it cannot do. An example of a distorted plain relation is the fraction. The fraction is based upon the illusion that once can be divided by a number greater than itself, which cannot be done in reality, and since anything based upon illusion is false, the fraction is both unprofitable and misleading because it is false, and consequently it may be struck from the record. In reality the fraction is nothing but a label when it occurs as a number and a metaphor when it is used as a name. In other words I may be metaphorically portioning out one third of a loaf of bread to a friend or I may be labelling it as such in order to conceal my greed because in fact I should have given a whole loaf.

*

We have learned a number of things here about certain numbers, and a catalogue of those things will be appended for the sake of orderliness. In the meantime it is best to learn these things as the need for them arises.

An example of a true equation has been given. An example of an extant equation, such as the human likeness of man and god, will now be demonstrated. The essence of man is perceived to be humanity, while the essence of god is perceived to lie in perception itself. The humanity of god resides in an act which has historical validity. The significance of this act is a source of

4

strength and its availability depends solely and entirely on the faculty of historical perception, and not at all on any factual reliability of the act itself. Whether or not this act occurred therefore is a perfectly useless question, since only within perception itself, as it springs from the human essence and as it voluntarily diminishes from signifiable view, can the unlimited conclusion be drawn which insists upon its own basis which was divinely created. The essence of god cannot be perpetrated, since that would presume to exclude him, and it cannot be extricated, since that would be an attempt to tempt him. Consequently it must be allowed to be effected by its own cause, which in the case of perception is the stimulus of pain. Why this is so is of no concern here and is explained in ample clarity in the Science of god. The divinity of man is not effected by its own cause at all, but issues in response to man's efforts. These efforts may not be predisposed, since that would divide them, and they may not be artificial, since that would render them intemperate, and to that degree effete. Only the utmost effort of man, and in no way unbalanced by promiscuity, achieves his divinity and brings him total and permanent satisfaction. In other words his efforts must be totally allied to nature and infallibly suited to human nature if they are to be both realized and established. Now in this real establishment of nature and of human nature through man's efforts, god's humanity is wholly unfolded and personally maintained. The same case may be stated in that through God's efforts as an act, his personality became human, and that from then on the historical significance of that act permeated all perception to the degree that perception existed at all, and grew to its fullness wherever perception was given full scope and was not hindered by ignorance and stupidity nor supererogated because of foolish zeal or idle protest, so that now this divine personality inhabits the earth and multiplies. This demonstrates our example of an extant equation, which is perceived and not comprehended.

A relation engenders life. It does this by means of concept and sense data. We never need to speak of sense data in the singular because they cannot be counted in any case and because the word refers to an immeasurable quantity. Concept we may speak of unpreceded by an article because it stands for measurement itself.

Relation and measurement are antinomies. This means that the same thing is named by each of them, but that the names have opposite derivation. The name relation for instance is derived from the conjoinment of two or more articles, while the name measurement is derived from the process of distinguishing something which is not whole for the purpose of making it whole. When we have antinomies we are able to make them serve each other. In the present case measurement serves relation in the capacity of concept, while relation serves measurement as sense data.

Antipodes give evidence of each other's position. The position of a number refers to its station in the decimal system. The position of the number one for instance is central, and the position of the number ten is peripheral. All other numbers between one and ten have a station in the decimal system peculiar to themselves. The station of two is conjunctional. The station of nine is proportional. The station of eight is constitutional. The station of three is internal. The station of four is eternal. The station of seven is temporal. The station of six is logical, and the station of five is final. Only in the cases of the numbers one and ten can we not freely interchange the term's position and station, since in the case of a central position in a system, for that position also to be stationary, the periphery of the system must coincide with it, otherwise the central position only approaches the stationary as an ideal and cannot be truly given the name of that ideal. In the same way, for the peripheral position to be stationary it must be coincidental with the central one, otherwise it only approximates the stationary as a model and cannot be given its name in fact. But if the peripheral position is actually coincidental with the central one, the system eclipses in any case, and the entire difference between position and station becomes meaningless for that occurrence. In the same way, if the central position should actually coincide with the peripheral one, the system is realized, and the difference between position and station has lost all importance. The distinction between the position and the station of a number is therefore only preserved for the purpose of identifying the system which is about to eclipse and the system which has been realized.

Only one difficulty remains to be cleared up. This is the difference between the system which is realized and the system which has been realized. The latter may not be real at present, although it must have been real at one time. We refer to such a system as a minimal one. The maximal system refers to the one which is presently real.

The decimal system is a logical one. It relates number in a tenfold manner. The proper use of this system allows us to employ numbers in terms of each other and on the basis of a tenfold scale.

A scale is a standard of measurement. What we do according to a scale is metrically limited. The peculiar application of metric limits permits the manipulation of pure quantity.

The tenfold scale makes possible implicit adjustment and explicit alignment. Adjustment is a function of fit, and alignment is an expression of concurrence. Implicit adjustment makes that fit which shares common property. Explicit alignment expresses concurrence virtually. The virtual expression of concurrence as explicit alignment and the fit in terms of common property due to implicit adjustment together make up the value of the tenfold scale.

The value of mathematics is beauty, and that beauty which is totally useful in that it has a good purpose. This beauty is instrumental in that it breaks down all resistance to the truth, and it is effective in that it supports fully all real growth and in that it is the only permanent foundation of all growth in reality. Therefore we say that growth and destruction are its vectors.

A vector is either a direction of force or an attraction of energy. As a direction of force it is formally constituted and substantially based. As an attraction of energy it is substantially shaped and conditionally formed. Conditional form and substantial shape are areas of vector analysis. Formal constitution and basic substance, which are the same as constitutional form and substantial basis, are eras of vector synthesis.

An era consists of a sum of periods. Each period is an impression of conventional time. The sum of all periods is referred to as the present moment, or as now. Now is the era of eternal time, which is the summation of all of conventional time. It is the present moment which allows this time to be understood. This is also the time which always was and always will be. It is the time according to which all things happen. It can be absolutely foretold and not at all predicted, because its realm is the quintessence of human essence and because according to it things happen habitually. Whatever is foretold therefore must either be seen as a fragment of universal occurrence, historically told or scientifically stated, or else not at all. This is the time which fulfils itself now, and which can never be superseded, since it occurs with ultimate finality. Those things which have not yet happened in this time must eventually happen in it, because this time embraces all things and all manner of thing. The mathematical sign which stands for it is the letter t.

An area is a locality of space. It is that space which has been predetermined and marked. Every area has an outline. The outline limits the area's expanse. Every area also has a surface. The surface limits the area's extension. Given its outline and surface an area is completely defined.

A plane is an area whose outline and surface are unlimited. The sum total of all planes is a sphere. The study of planes is called geometry.

A line is an area which extends and whose outline is ruled. Given the rule of its outline and its extension, a line is accurately defined.

The sum total of all lines is called a globe. The study of lines is called geodesy. It takes the globe as its final object and begins with the unlimited line, which is a point. Every point has coordinates and parameters. Its coordinates set it, and its parameters proceed from it. The distance between two points cannot be measured, but only assumed. Any three points map out an angle. Any four points describe a figure. No more than two points can come to lie in the same direction. A point must not be confused with a dot. No more than three points can lie on the same angle. An angle must not be confused with a corner. A figure must be described by at least four points. It must not be confused with a design.   is a design.

A circle is defined as a shaped line. It depends only upon itself for direction. An ellipse is defined as a formed line. It depends on the circle for direction. The circle is direction incarnate. It cannot be any further defined. There is no such thing as the ellipse. A square is a patterned line. It depends only upon itself for attraction. The attracted line differs from the directed line in that it follows a course of events, while the directed line precedes a course of events. The square is the pattern. A rectangle is a line which depends upon the square for attraction.

There is no such thing as the rectangle. All lines are either directed or attracted.

A curve is a line which approximates a circle. When it is directed it is concave, when it is attracted it is convex. All curves are either concave or convex.

That curve which most nearly approximates a circle lies within the confines of that circle. It is said to be circular. That curve which least nearly or most distantly approximates a circle lies within the boundary of that circle. It is said to be acircular. Between the confines and the boundary of a circle all curves which approximate it are to be found.

An angle is a line which approximates a square. That angle which most nearly approximates a square lies within the pattern of that square. It is said to be patterned. That angle which least nearly or most distantly approximates a square lies within the design of that square. It is said to be designed. Within the pattern and the design of the square all angles which approximate it are to be found.

While mathematics involves illusion it is not sound. Extinct mathematics laboured under the illusion that substance needed to be either visible or invisible. For visible substance it invented its systems and attempted through them and by means of them to render that substance invisible. For invisible substance it made up signs and attempted in terms of these and on the basis of them to render that substance visible. The extinct mathematical problem was classically one of an interchange of credible possibilities. Whatever had become too familiar was adopted as matter, and whatever had become strange enough was extracted as form. Then the former was delightfully transformed into the latter. It struck only the most detached philosophers that what was going on here had as its purpose and ambition the possession in all privacy of an ideal beauty which could then be toyed with at leisure far from the madding crowd. Those philosophers then proceeded to devise a new system, one of their own, and in reaction to the other, heightening once again the effect of this fickle beauty, which could only be enjoyed in the bedroom of the imperfect imagination, because outside in reality her demands became outrageous and really quite unacceptable to the gentleman of learning. But this child of fancy must tend eventually to burst into flame, burning the perspiring hands which would have grasped her. For this reason this present mathematics, which is not extinct but live, might seem at first to be somewhat painful.

We go on then, nevertheless, to further consideration of the decimal system. It is a logical system which uses the number ten as a categorical device. This must be understood completely. A device is a product of invention. It stems from the intellect in response to a particular need. What this need was or is can only result in idle speculation. Of importance is only that the necessity underlying the invention of the device is recognized as a fact, and that one may deduce therefore that the application of the device leads to a perfection.

As soon as that perfection has been reached, the device becomes obsolete. In obsolescence it has use as a category. This means that it is now strictly an adjunct of order. As such it has qualities of observation and an objective being of its own which must be reckoned with. If one forgets this, any matter which is subordinate to the category will to that degree become obsolescent. With the categorical device obsolete and the subordinate matter obsolescent, the result is the cessation of reason, which is usually referred to as senility.

While reason is viewed either in an anticipatory fashion to the intellect or else in postponement to it, it depends upon the intellect, either in terms of categories and in subjection to experience, or else on the basis of intellectual substance and with experience as its object. This state of affairs existed in Western philosophy prior to the advent of the philosophy of Immanuel Kant. Thinking inclined either towards the metaphysical school where feeling remained suspect, or else it veered towards the empirical camp where feeling had good reason to become increasingly less secure.

In the philosophy of Kant reason is not viewed any more, in one manner or the other, but it is seen, and consequently understood, as the basis of intellect which it can be. Also in that philosophy it was then interpreted, and as a basis of the intellect which it must be. The former step was an incomparable increase in knowledge. The latter step, due to the interpretative faculty of the intelligence, amounted to a securing of that gained increase of knowledge upon a permanent basis.

It remained to comprehend reason as the guide of the growing intelligence which it might be. This has been done in our philosophy, where the growing intelligence gives the structure to physical being, where physical being entails the process of continuing creation which in turn involves a detailed assimilation of structure in terms of structure as an end in itself, and where reason assumes the role of a medium preparing for the possibility of all things.

Reason as this medium lends itself to total representation in terms mathematical. This representation orders all things, not insofar as they are, but insofar as they are possible. It is not a system, but the system. It underlies all other systems, whether logical, solar, or psychosomatic. We can discuss it therefore in general even though we will not be able to give examples.

There is no such thing as a mathematical system or as the mathematical system. There is this system however, which in mathematical terms represents all the order of all possible things. It relies upon no constant. In order to be understood it must be approached by an imagination not less than perfect. The imagination cannot be perfected by means of this system, as it can be through study of other systems. We must say therefore that mathematics is a study for those who have arrived at a certain state of insight, and who's imagination does not any more vacillate between intemperance and merely external significance.

This system unites emotions, passions, thought, strength and perception in one single experience and bases them wholly upon themselves. There is no element of hypothesis to be found in it. By the same token does it not commence at all from theory. It gives the indication of reality which leads directly to its appreciation, and it unites all matters natural in such a way that they may be treated as real objects.

The mathematical terms which make up this system are all special. They cannot be adopted for any other purpose except to achieve reality. Therefore they are also called real terms. Whatever is fixed in them stands for all time, and whatever is based upon them retains its validity anywhere.

The nature of a mathematical term is that it is defined from within. This means that its definition rests upon the application of the term, and that it can neither be understood nor created outside of the term's use. The use of the mathematical term is metamorphic. It changes that which is shapeless into an attribute of shape. Shape however is entirely composed of attributes, and whatever has shape is to that degree distinct and unique. Shape itself is entirely unique and distinct.

The possible thing is most readily shaped. In order to be shape it needs merely to be linked to its attributes. Since the possible thing approaches its attributes without identifying with them, the link which is necessary to give it shape amounts to an inversion of that thing's universal quantity. Of course the link itself cannot be pointed out, since it is nothing else, but it can be installed. This installation is referred to as the miraculous power.

The miracle, which is an instantaneous realization of the possible, is not performed, but instated. Let us presume for instance that it is possible for an animal to speak. This means that this animal carries within itself the power of speech, and that all the attributes of speech, which would release this power, are within access of the animal's faculties of comprehension. The miracle then consists in a unification of all the animal's efforts in terms of its latent powers of speech not for any purpose nor in response to an end but inwardly conceived and brought to fruition entirely on the grounds of its own spontaneous effects. The conditions for such an event must be perfect. Perfect conditions entail an exact replica of that which they would bring about. Therefore

13

in the present case the necessary conditions contain all the faculties of speech concentrated into one single facet of reality and supported by the special power of understanding.

The effect of the special mathematical term is whole. The whole effect carries over the essence of being and applies it in existence. Each mathematical term does what more than one do, and what all of them do, which is the system. The system differs from the single term as the whole differs from the one. One must always be whole, but it is not the whole. The whole on the other hand is always one, and it is the one. The attribute of wholeness, in other words entails the attribute of oneness, and the attribute of oneness is a detail of the attribute of wholeness.

The special mathematical term cannot be imagined. It contains however that which creates the image. It contains the reflex of the imagination. This reflex is the same in whichever mathematical term one cares to deal with, and with the number of such terms available the power of the reflex increases, but not its nature. The reflective power of all mathematical terms taken together, which is the power of the system, is infinite. The reflexive power of a single term, or of a number of terms, is purely quantitative in size. For this quantity to be qualified it must be distributed logically. A logical distribution is according to measurement and growth. Factors of measurement are limits whose tangible presence may be known. Factors of growth are limits whose tangible presence may be understood. The sum total of all growth and measurement factors makes up the system's environment.

The environment of the system cannot be defined of course, it is both infinite and finite, depending on the category under which it is approached and also depending upon whether or not it is approached categorically at all. Five separate instances may be delineated. There is first of all the systematic response to the environment, which results in a product. This product is unique in that it contains nothing systematic at all. It may be referred

14

to as a medium. It is neither an impression nor an expression of anything, and it points to nothing outside of itself. Therefore it cannot be interpreted. Secondly there is interaction with the environment. Since the system and its environment are always in balance, interaction between the two is entirely devoid of reaction. It is registered as an order or as a plan. When it is registered as an order, we may conclude that the interaction was systematically stimulated. This is so because order and stimulus are cause and effect of each other, and because an environmental stimulus does not come about. When the interaction is registered as a plan however, we may infer that it was environmentally absorbed. The plan is then a relation between experience and action, and the experience rather than the action has been given the upper hand. Both the response to the environment, which was first discussed, and the interaction between system and environment, are categorically conceived and propounded, and the category under which they have occurred is nowhere in evidence. It is taken up entirely into the process of response or interaction, so that ultimately it has become one with the product and with the order or plan. Thirdly we have to do with an impingement upon the environment by the system and this results in another system, which is however not related in any way to the system which generated it. Such an impingement upon the system's environment is categorical in its approach of the environment but not as it makes contact with it. During contact a category is produced, but in total independence of the new system, and this new category is then available as an adjunct of the system which was generated.

The fourth instance is the behaviour of the system as a receptacle or recipient of the environment. It is one or the other depending upon whether an object is desired or whether a subject is to be expressed. In either case the environment is perceived as a whole and it is allowed to impress the system as a whole. This impression then brings about the desired object or subject.

The subject will be created in response to the impression of the whole environment, and the object will be made as a representation of the whole environment's impression. The fifth instance is the system's accommodation of the environment. Such an accommodation occurs either as an appropriation, when the environment is viewed as a flux, or else as an assimilation, when it is understood as substance.

The understanding of environment as substance is a very recent achievement of the human brain. Before it could be accomplished it was necessary to adapt reason to life, and to eternal life. Once reason had become local and temporal at once, there was no more need for the intellect to prepare, partially or completely, for the likelihood of reason and consequently the entire intellect could turn towards the environment and face it, discriminating for once between substance and matter, and at the same time distinguishing, as separate entities, form and shape.

Illusion goes into the original process of naming something. Ultimately however the name is free of illusion. In both cases it is called a name. But only in the latter case is it also at the same time a concept. To identify the latter from the former we call it the real name and the former the original name.

The original and the real name can never be two different words, but they must be one and the same word. In the case of the original name the word is described. In the case of the real name that same word describes. The change which occurs from the former to the latter case is called the epistemological process. The word which is described has nothing in common with that same word when it describes. We have come here to a negative understanding of what the word in itself amounts to. It can be the same word, but it may have nothing in common with it. Now two things which have nothing in common with each other cannot participate in the same process. They may however undergo the same operation. The process and the operation differ from each other in the same way as the described and the describing word, if they are the same word. Here we come to a negative understanding of what time in itself is. Even though the process and the operation both take time, they have nothing in common. The contradiction of course is illusory. But even though the original and the real name, though having nothing in common, are yet the same word, the process and the operation, also having nothing in common, are not the same anything. In fact they are true opposites. This does not mean that one is not the other, which would be apparent opposition, but that they exclude each other, wholly and in ever respect. This then is the true meaning of addition and summation, that things which mutually exclude each other wholly and in every respect are counted and accounted for under an artificial concept or upon an illusory basis. When five apples and five apples are added to make ten apples, this addition proceeds upon the illusory basis that all apples are alike and the same, when in fact they have nothing in common, and when five apples and five pears are summed up as ten fruits, this summation operates under the artificial concept of the fruit, which suggests that apples and pears have the same attributes in one fashion of another, when in fact the have nothing in common. It is not event rue that some apples have the same appearance. No two apples can be found to have the same appearance. Nor is it true that any apple and any pear can be conceived to be similar and the same in any manner or form. No two fruits can be conceived to be the same. In the case of the summation of apples and pears as fruits it is the intellect which supplies an artificial concept, not by operating, but by refraining from operation while the summation is made, and in other words by not participating in the operation which goes on so that the sum may be drawn. In the case of the addition of apples and apples it is the imagination which contributes the illusory basis of the apple, even though there is no such thing as the apple, and it manages this not by proceeding, but by refraining from taking part in the process of the addition, so that a sum may be arrived at.

Both the process of addition and the operation of summation end in a sum, but exactly that this sum is an end means that its occurrence in both cases does not contradict but in fact corroborate the statement of the process and the operation as true opposites. Only true opposites can have the same end. This does not mean that they have something in common either, since an end is nothing that can be shared in to begin with. If true opposites however do have something in common they are called real opposites. For opposites to be real, in other words, they must exclude each other, and they must have something in common.

We will clarify this point more explicitly since it may seem to harbour a contradiction. Two things which have nothing in common do not necessarily exclude each other, as true opposites. We saw this in the case of the word, where the same word was both an original name and a real name, where the two names had nothing at all in common. On the other hand, when two things exclude each other, as true opposites, this does not mean that they must have nothing in common, but only that they do not have their natural essence in common; but if they did have their natural essence in common they could not be two things but would have to be one and the same thing. That two or more things can exclude each other and yet have something in common is seen in the case of all real opposites.

Which brings us to the point that more than two things can exclude each other, in the sense that all the apples in a large basket full of apples exclude each other, but that no more than two things can be true opposites, since opposition implies duality. This tells us something about subtraction.

When we take away from a number of things, we do not diminish that number, but we simply find a different place for those things which we take away. Subtraction is neither an operation nor a process unless a conventional area of concern is first agreed upon. If this area adheres to usual dimensions, such as in the case of subtracting ten from fifteen, an operation rakes place, and a result is retained, which result lies in the original area of concern. If the area of concern is an experimental one however, such as when we subtract ten apples from fifteen apples, or if it is an expression of our experience, such as when we subtract this from that, given this and that at the moment, then subtraction is a process and the result is called a remainder which lies in a totally new area of concern with respect to the original one. A remainder is a result too, but it is a particular kind of result, with unique attributes different from those of the original number of things.

Subtraction and addition, like most other mathematical operations and processes, have for so long gone on either in the realm of number divorced from nature or else in nature divorced from reality that they have become very adulterated, abused and misunderstood. Extinct mathematics attempted to achieve a system of number and of numerical operation which would express the void. Why one would wish to express the void rather than something to fill it is difficult to apprehend now, but the attempt to achieve the impossible is after all the hallmark of extinction. Number in the realm of unreal or false nature takes on the cloak of prestidigitation and magic without being able to work real magic, which is miraculous, and as such it fascinates those who crave mystery for its own sake and who would isolate themselves in esoteric studies so as to escape from the common crowd. The study of number divorced from nature creates no end of complexity and of mental gymnastics, all of it contrary to good sense and of course of no use except in rationalization as a temptation to be overcome. Those who are attracted by the acrobatics of empty numbers are advised not to take part since the crowd is egotistical and the equipment grows increasingly faulty as the show progresses. Reasons for participating in this nonsense are usually a confusion of complexity with pro-

19

fundity, and a desire for aesthetic purity which has become misdirected and has in fact turned into a search of sensual reality, which is a thing contrary to reason and joy.

When number pertains to nature and includes nature in reality it is in itself a concrete thing and not any more abstract. In the same way of course name must be an increment of history, and that history must include all of time, present, past and future, if name is not to become an empty sound and a dead letter. In extinct mathematics name had become a sign, and signs were interpreted in terms of each other, and this gradually resulted in nonsense names which only retained an application insofar as they were misused. Since the reality of time was conceived rather than understood, history always remained separated from time, and consequently the name could not achieve its purpose and became useless, either as a device which became old-fashioned, or as meaningless content which had lost the power of myth. Nonsense names and useless names correspond to false number and to empty number as the negative limitations of mathematical relation.

We come now to a rather wonderful aspect of mathematics, which is its influence as myth. Myth is defined as the good and purposeful application of time. This definition is clarified as soon as we point out that the good application not of time is not necessarily purposeful, and if it is not, we are dealing with created history, which is a recreation of time, and cannot be called myth. By the same token is the purposeful application of time not necessarily good, since it may be merely right, in which case we are dealing with recorded history, which is a record of the appearances of time, and again cannot be called myth. For the application of time to be both good and purposeful it is necessary that time is observed as life and then abstracted from life so that it may become concrete as eternal life. While it is observed as life there is no distinction yet between useful and temporary and between that which is possessed and that which is given.

20

For life to become valuable and meaningful rather than mere life, which had neither value nor meaning, time is perfectly abstracted, and this again is one of the applications of mathematics, when it results in myth.

Myth is life when it is demonstrated in eternity. Myth and reality do not exclude each other, but myth is reality before it has fully embraced nature. Reality does not infer nature, but only the truth. Reality completely separate from nature, as we know, is not possible. Reality and nature as one is the kingdom, which is presently being established upon the earth. As reality involves more of nature, right to the point where it becomes one with it, which is the end of the world, it is referred to as myth. Since the world has come to an end, we can clearly distinguish myth from established reality, and we can see that all myth has only this one essence, which is the establishment of man in reality, and even though the world is no more, myth nevertheless survives and serves man, not any more now as an involvement of nature with reality, but as an indication of that involvement which eventually became total.

When we say that something is mythic or mythical we are saying first of all that it gives evidence of systematic universality, and secondly that it is human and alive. Just as nature is inconceivable without man and as reality is inconceivable without nature, so is man inconceivable without history, and history without myth. But history must not be confused with myth. history deals with time as man perceives it and experiences it. Myth on the other hand is itself time, concrete and in progress, and, since it is concrete, of course eternal.

Ever since the beginning of time, myth, which was made, had to precede any history since time must be concrete before it can be perceived and experienced. Ever since the beginning of time also man could not know of his existence unless he perceived and experienced time. But though myth must precede history, history does not precede human self-awareness, but

21

occurs simultaneous with it. One is unthinkable without the other. It is the same with the soul of man, where, of the will and the intellect, one must precede the other, while the conscience occurs simultaneously with the one which is the reflex of the other. Whether we look into the soul of man or at universal life, we see one and the same thing, and know that it is what it seems to be, which is true.

Having briefly set forth how myth fits into the order of things and what it is in essence, we continue to demonstrate its mathematical behaviour.

To say that myth behaves is to demonstrate behaviour itself. Before we even know what it is which behaves, and given that behaviour goes on, we know that an agent exists and that this agent is human. To speak of the behaviour of a rat is to describe the human being which is attempting to see and to observe. It is the human being as an agent however, and only as an agent, which lends itself to a discussion of behaviour in itself.

To say that myth behaves mathematically is the same as to say that all behaviour is at bottom and in purpose mythical. The very faculty of speech, which is essentially human, is a facet of behaviour and mathematical in kind. This means that speech is a mythical creation, and that it is automatically mythical creation. It is for this reason that all speech, whether it is comprehensible or not, may be believed when it is taken at face value, and perfect communication is just such an acceptance of speech as automatic myth. Another facet of behaviour are the physical movements of man as an agent. However the human agent acts or reacts, he will do so automatically in terms of physical reality, and his movements will be mathematical and mythical. They will be mathematical in that they will coincide, no matter how complex or premeditated and in matter how spontaneous or ideal, with the universal laws of behaviour, and they will be mythical in that their intent and reason, no matter how conscious and aware and no matter whether conscious or aware at all, will be the establishment of man in the kingdom upon the earth.

Now of course the facets of behaviour are infinite in number and indefinite in name, since the human agent is an incarnate thing and since its physical powers are not at all limited, stemming from the very essence of being which is humanity. On the other hand it must be reminded that all aspects of myth taken as a whole make up what is known as the Son of Man, which cannot be given another name. It is the Son of Man in whom all myth dwells. Every aspect of myth taken separately distinguishes the Son in a certain way, and each aspect of myth taken at a time points to his essence. The essence of the Son of Man is love, and it is this love which generates and produces whatever has the character of myth or contains its elements. The character of myth is the expression of human quality and the impression of human experience. The elements of myth are the various quantities of human personality and the diverse effects of that personality demonstrated.

The system is the mental reproduction of the kingdom. All that is in the kingdom, which will eventually include all things, is mythically reproduced in the system. The system is the myth. As the system it reveals the order and as the myth it conserves that order. As the system it reflects the kingdom and as the myth it shields and protects the kingdom. No one can know the myth unless he is in the kingdom, and no one can understand the system unless he knows the myth. Knowledge of the myth precedes the understanding of the system, and the entrance into the kingdom coincides with the knowledge of the myth. The difference between myth and the myth is clarified by the acceptance of the fact that belief in myth leads into the kingdom, but that the myth must be understood from within the kingdom, where all myth contributes to that understanding.

One principle underlies all knowledge in mathematics, and it is the indivisibility of that which is one. Whatever is one cannot be divided. To be one is not a condition, nor a state, nor a situation, nor a relationship, but it is nothing else, and no other name can be found for it, and it cannot be otherwise described. When two or more things are one it means that they cannot be distinguished one from the other. Only their mere appearance may differ. Criteria of oneness are in fact the independence of mere appearance, and its opposite, the causal involvement of the truth. These two are opposite in the sense that only one of the two may be observed at a time. Nevertheless both exist simultaneously. The independence of mere appearance may be observed as an epiphenomenon of change or else as an impress of order. In both cases appearance and individuality are said to mesh perfectly. In other words, what seems to be is always in truth the case. The casual involvement of the truth may be observed as a mark of time or else as an indication of invisibility. By a mark of time is meant that by which the progress of time may be gauged and which is meant to serve that express purpose. Indications of invisibility are given wherever and whenever the truth is revealed in absolute perfection, and they are what is referred to as striations of time, on the basis of which that which is invisible may be apprehended.

Upon this principle of oneness, stating that whatever is one cannot be divided, is based the principle of division, which states that whatever can be divided, can be infinitely divided.

And from these two principles follows the third, stating that whatever is not one and cannot be divided is a thing. This does not define a thing however. A thing must be defined in terms of all other things, and the number of things which exist is always finite. Those things which do not exist do not concern us, and they are generally referred to as nothing. Nothing can be defined as all those things which do not exist, and whose essence may or may not be known to us. Since existence precedes essence, if a thing does not exist and its essence is known to us, we know that it must have ceased to exist, which allows us to differenti-

24

ate between nothing and dead things, the latter being the former, but the former not necessarily the latter.

The fourth principle arises from the former three and states that all things must be accounted for. This implies that the existence of the individual thing depends upon and is interdependent with the existence of all things.

The fifth principle follows from the fourth, and states that the existence of all things may be known.

While the fourth principle contains an imperative, the fifth one dos not. That is why we say that the knowledge of the existence of things is free. It is based solely upon the human will. The philosophy of A. Schopenhauer illustrates this principle in all its effectiveness. It does not however totally demonstrate it. In order to demonstrate totally that the existence of all things may be known, the human will must not only be free but also wholly dedicated. Only then does it become apparent what it means that the existence of all things may be known, but that it neither can nor cannot be known. Were it true that the existence of all things can be known, then the mere possibility of that knowledge would suffice on the part of the thing to be known that knowledge is gained from it. This however is not the case. Neither is it true on the other hand that the existence of all things cannot be known, simply because it may. What then has to be added to the possibility of the knowledge of the existence of things so that this knowledge becomes definitely available? It is the advocacy of time. Now is the time that the existence of all things may be known. Until now the possibility of this knowledge was understood, and all knowledge proceeded from that possibility. Or, to put it otherwise, for a time it was understood that the knowledge of the existence of all things was possible, but now we know that the existence of all things may be known.

Possibility does not imply actuality, but only eventual actuality, given the necessary power. Although something cannot be eternally possible, it may certainly be possible and not actual for all time. For the possible to come about, one thing is necessary, which is a tribute of power. A tribute of power has neither source nor origin, but only an end, and this end is always its attribute. Any attribute may be understood as an achieved quantity of power, and only if it is understood in this way can it also be released for the express purpose of bringing about the possible. Again we will repeat and stress that no attribute must be understood this way, since it can also be understood in many other ways, and also that in order to bring about the possible it is not true that the attribute must be understood in this way, since that would imply a necessary link between this way of understanding and the brought about possibility, which link is not the case; but it is true that every attribute may be understood in this way, and if it is, that which is possible may certainly be brought about. It may be frustrating to some that what is being emphasized here cannot be neatly done away with in a term or two or perhaps even given a private name of its own. But be it known to those who have laboured in the name of extinction that their labours have by no means been wasted but that what we are presently emphasizing is the one thing which would not bow to extinction, and it has become the cornerstone of the edifice of life.

The five principles of mathematics have been set forth. Their relationship to each other has been touched upon. The next step is to map out for each of these principles an area of inference.

Beginning with the fifth, which states that the existence of all things may be known, we infer primarily that knowledge which springs from the existence of things can also be understood, and that its understanding depends upon the intellect, upon the free intellect, and upon the freely applied intellect. In the case of the intellect freedom of application means a reliance upon the wholly dedicated will and upon nothing else. This is referred to as the intellect's voluntary reliance, and it implies absolute responsibility. Decisions are therefore always made relative to the absolute, and choice is not only free, but absolutely determined. judgment on the other hand is never a function which is separate and distinct, but it participates finally. It is the judgment which was foretold, and which has now come into action. As an inclusion of action it not only separates what is good from what is not good, but it also distinguishes that which is good in itself from that which is good for a purpose or for a reason. It does not separate the good from the bad however, since it simply does not concern itself with what is bad and rejects it outright along with all that which is not good. Neither does it separate right from wrong, since all such distinction has come to an end with the coming to an end of the world, so that all which was right then is now finally judged according to whether it is merely right and therefore without value, or whether it is properly right and therefore useful – or whether it is eminently right and therefore noble. No notice is being taken of that which was then wrong. That which is distinctively useful, meaning that use is its primary function, is immediately put to use without any further ceremony. That which is distinctively noble, meaning that nobility is its foremost quality, is right away given its definitive position. That which has no value is used as raw material, meaning that it supports the mere body and makes up the weight of the earth. This is what is meant when the earth is referred to as a footstool.

The area of inference which extends from the fifth principle of mathematics includes then the final judgment and the voluntary intellect, and implies the distinguishment of raw material, of the noble and of the useful on one hand, and the perpetration of the extrinsically and intrinsically good on the other. That which is good in itself needs no further attention, because it has become part of the kingdom. That which is extrinsically good is either applied so as to become part of the kingdom, if it is good for a reason or else it is adopted as part of the kingdom, if it is good for a purpose. That which is neither good in itself nor good for a reason or a purpose cannot be good at all. The kingdom consists only of things which are good and of things which are right. It is composed of the former and it contains the latter. The one single action which unites all things of the kingdom is a special love.

The area of inference of the fourth principle of mathematics, which principle states that all things must be accounted for, includes on one hand the categorical imperative of reason, and on the other it opens the field of experiment to the active conscience. By experiment here is meant no idle manipulation of appearances to see what will happen, but the intelligent extension of limits and the expansion of recognized bounds, not on the basis of or in line with reason, but always very carefully apprehended so as to avoid the perverse and the absurd. Perverse is that experiment which presupposes its own perimeter of expectation and tempts existence by artificially unbalancing the forces of nature. Such experimentation is cowardly and leads automatically to the ruin of the senses. Experimentation is absurd when exceptional conditions or states are treated on a par with the norm so as to make them yield information which has been anticipated. Such experiments are existentially dishonest because they try to coerce nature into a pattern which it cannot fit. The mind as a result soon inclines now towards the ill-adjusted and now towards the grotesque, and eventually takes on the shape of its weakness and addiction. Experimentation which remains constantly conscientious however is eventually piloted by the conscience, which separates then, previous to the test by reason, that which is possible from that which is probable, leaving that which is likely; whereupon it separates that which is merely likely from such likelihood which resides in the truth, which is called the category. The category is a definitive term, beyond which nothing worth knowing exists. It may be broken down into categories, of course, which in turn may be grouped as one sees fit and as best serves one's purpose but beyond the category of existence only the chaotic and the charismatic may be found, and nothing worth knowing is to be gained there. We say that the conscience ponders the probable, that it contemplates the possible, that it weighs the likely and that it screens the category, all by way of experimentation. Each of these steps may be fully described. Pondering the probable, the conscience becomes aware of its content and isolates it. Upon isolation it separate automatically into matter and substance. The substance is immediately assimilated, which adds strength to the process, and the matter is sifted, so that its intrinsic make-up becomes recognizable. This is then contemplated. Form and shape become apparent if they exist, and that which is formless and shapeless is judged to be either merely effective, in which case it is stored, or else contiguous, in which case it is abstracted. Form and shape are then weighed. Whatever the case, whether the form is fitting or not and whether the shape is precise or premature, dictates the nature of the advance. The conscience does not respond to the misshapen and to the poorly formed. It is repulsed by a positive lack of form, and the real absence of shape inhibits it, which registers as shame or as guilt depending on whether the will is passive or active. It is because of these secondary emotions that the experimental process often miscarries, ending in the attempt and the fragment, simply because initially the conscience was not fully suited to its task, either due to a lack of preparation through neglect of trial or else as a result of insufficient practical stamina because of energy not proficiently invested. The outcome of the weighing process should be that all available limitation is purely and simply used up. Naturally to the uninitiated this must at first be a startling experience. When no guidelines are left, a very special quality is required if that next step is to be taken which will reveal the as yet unknown. There is only one name for this special quality, and it is faith. Only in a medium of spotless faith will the new dimension open and will the archaic become available. Only in a setting of otherwise unproven trust will the not yet logical be made serviceable and will the static accept the breath of life. Then the terminal work of the conscience begins. The category is always the same. It may be described as the temporary appearance of time, as that which is commonly measured by clocks and pictured in segments of years, days, minutes and so on. Important is that it cannot be pointed out or interpreted. It must be accepted as is if at all and there is neither time nor space for selection or choosing. If choice at this stage is insisted upon, the senses are destroyed. If one perseveres in selecting only that which seems to fit the familiar pattern, the wits are dulled. The first products of the categorical conscience will always at first seem unworthy. They will be awkward in shape and form and totally strange in appearance. But these are the harbingers of the best which the human being is capable of. If one only accepts them in good faith and casts all justification to the winds, one will discover after a time that one's conscience has been blessed with a special peace indeed. This will be so because the conscience will finally be doing that which it was created for in the beginning. The screening process is merely a matter of holding out in the storm, of enduring before the seemingly unaccountable, of suffering the approach of the new, the unfamiliar and the strange, and of supporting the conscience energetically as it advances. All else either happens as in a dream, or in perfect submission, or in beneficial violence, or in ecstasy, or as a wonderful mystery. Which of these five concurs is of little importance and only of incidental interest since it has no bearing at all on the child which is being delivered. The clown arrives in a mood of abstraction; the new day dawns to the accompaniment of laughter; the composition of the dance occurs while the dragon snores; reality is founded upon images wrested from a nightmare; a normal meal is taken while suddenly the spirit enters the flesh. In all five cases the one cannot be linked with the other, except in the manifold acceptance of new life.

When we look at the categorical imperative of reason, which is included in the area of inference of the fourth principle, it reveals itself as a paradox. On one hand it seems to dictate the very law of necessity, and on the other, if we only act accordingly, it frees us once and for all from the very same law. The apparent contradiction lies in the contradictoriness of appearances. What seems to be one way turns out the opposite of what it did not at all seem, but what it seemed and what it did not seem were in the beginning not at all opposite.

The categorical imperative of reason states the conditions and requirements under which absolute knowledge and perfect understanding may be gained. Those conditions and requirements are never repeated, never once during the eternal lifespan of the universe, and they are entirely inconstant. What is sometimes mourned as fleeting time or regretted as passing beauty is in fact the very essence of the universe, and it is as it is only because it must change in order to exist. Today it may exist wholly, for the first time uninhibited by man's senses as he assimilates meaning and finds it concordant with his own essence. For the first time since the beginning of time this surface of the material world has been penetrated by the intellect and its stuff has been uplifted by the will to the point where it becomes substantial. It is true that we cannot ask for more.

The categorical imperative of reason operates only insofar as reason is limited by itself. Self-limited reason is the idea of reason realized. The idea of reason reflects it as an attribute of nature and as the principal attribute of man. For this idea of reason to be realized, reason must become aware of itself. In this awareness it defines itself as the purpose of mortal life. As such it draws all matter into itself. Once reason has materialized it is not any more a faculty, but a power. The power of reason is next in greatness to the power of faith. While faith can work miracles, reason can work logic. Reason not only working logic, but comprehending itself in its work of logic, is not a power, but it is a

person. This is what personality means, that I is the free contribution of reason of itself to its work. The central element of the
person is authenticity. It arises from reason recognizing itself in
its work. Authenticity is the only guarantee of personality and
without authenticity the person does not exist. Originality has
nothing to do with personality at all. It is an increment of character. In the case of character reason does not enter into its work,
but it manipulates it from without. The categorical imperative
of reason is initiated by personality. Due to its authenticity the
person negates its opposite, which is the subject, and for this
negation to occur personality merely has to be. The negated subject implies the liberated object. The liberated object is one which
has become part of behaviour and which is entirely involved in
behaviour. It is still called an object, but now it is never unob-
served. No subject corresponds to the permanently observed object. The difference between such an object and a thing is that
the thing contains substance while the object does not. Therefore we say that the object is effete. The human body for example either a subject, or an object, or a liberated object. It is
also possible for the human body to be a thing. In that case it
contains substance and is eternal. The authentic personality creates for itself such a body which is a thing, and once that process has begun the imperfect body, which is subject or object, is
cast off. Only after this body has been cast off can the categorical imperative of reason be taken advantage of. At such a time
the body is the mind and the mind is the body while being is
human in essence. Taking advantage of the imperative amounts
to assenting to an eternal and continuing exchange of substance
between mind and body. Each time substance transfers from one
to the other it does work, and this work means first of all an
increase of that substance, forty, sixty, or one-hundredfold, depending upon the rate of exchange which is set by nature, and
then it means a corresponding manifestation of that substance

as it increases, which today is the establishment of the Kingdom of Heaven on earth, which is the establishment of the kingdom.

It is an imperative according to which reason applies its measure, and this imperative dictates the direction and attraction of action and passion. Because of its source, it would be absurd to suspect this imperative of being unreasonable. The imagination assists when we contemplate what it might be like when we do what must be done, given that the deed promises satisfaction and pleasure not of a higher degree than other possible action relative to it, but satisfaction and pleasure even of a higher nature. When we know that we must submit, and that we must wholly submit before we are to become wholly sovereign, our submission tends to involve a certain precipitation of the senses which reminds us of a cross between grace and ecstasy, between charm and exaltation, and we bow to our momentary debasement before the all in an unmitigated spirit of compassion with the all, which is a person like we are, and has suffered most fatefully so that we might arrive at the destiny. And what is most delightful to our fancy is the anticipation of our vain pride's removal without trace as a consequence of our exposure. For those who have decided for love rather than to be praised, the obstacle of this pride has become a most hateful thing, and the beauty which promises to reign in its absence fires them on to speedy dispatchment. If on the other hand they have chosen love rather than contentment, then their submission will surely find them out as objects deserving of comfort, and such a peace will enter their hearts that they will never again be lacking the resolve for what they decide, and then their contentment in love will be unbounded. There is a misery which can be inflicted by pure reason such as no experience has warned us about. To bear this misery out of love, and to endure in it, and to recall at the time how our nature must have strayed to become so estranged from reason, this is a work reserved only for those rare individuals who are chosen to commemorate the way for the sake of our appreciation. All valid

33

doctrine arises out of states of resignation before universal truth. But the voluntary and prepared and self-initiated subjection of the passions, of our thoughts, and even of our instincts, in short, of the will to the rule of reason, this means far more than doctrine, and it elicits the incomparable example, which can only persuade. The fire which burns us clean then is enough to take our breath away, and even after we have become purified once and for all, this fire remains with us and serves us as the element under the onslaught of which no vain resistance may hold.

Since the imperative of reason is categorical, it operates in absolute rest. This rest alone is a phenomenon to behold. It is a palpable state of physical existence. But in order to be effective it must be supported. This entails merely an awareness of it. Within this awareness the mind functions spontaneously. Because of it the body can grow, uninhibited and according to classical dimensions.

The term categorical implies the concept of the classical. That is classical which depends upon no outside force for its proportion. Its opposite is the irrational, which depends entirely upon outside force for proportion. Again we remind here that those things are opposites whose definitions exclude each other. The rational and the irrational are no more opposites than black and white are, which is not at all. Those things which negate each other are no opposites, but contradictions. When we ponder what is meant by classical proportions we come to an understanding of the rational, which is a case of classical proportionate meaning. Prior to the advent of the law's fulfilment, classical dimension, both in meaning and growth, represented the ideal of excellence. Whether human or cosmic, the nature of that ideal was strife and attainment, and whether it was described in terms of the ethical or represented as a sympathy of natural bodies, it always formed in one way or another the hub of the human wheel of progress. With the advent of the law's fulfilment the concentration upon this ideal by no means ceased. But while the ideal

34

previously served as a focus for the sake of collecting energy and measuring strength, it now became a decoy for the purpose of attracting all that energy which refused to meet the event of the law's fulfilment and channelling it to its own surcease; and it became a false image for the purpose of directing all that strength which denied the event of the law's fulfilment to its natural death. The ideal had turned into the principal instrument of extinction. All those who pursued the classical ideal, instead of accepting the new life, concerned themselves instead with inhibiting the process of death and of the dying of the old life, which death could not be avoided at any rate, but those who concerned themselves with the new life which came from the fulfilment of the law died to the old life without noticing it. All the extinct arts and sciences are in form and content an attempt to slow down that process which came to its speediest and most successful conclusion wherever it went unnoticed. Whenever the live arts showed promise of developing they were shut out by the faculty of reason because it could not cope with them. It was necessary for the faculty of reason to become the medium of reason before a live art could be nourished to maturity, which has occurred now. Live science had not even been attempted prior to reason becoming a medium.

It should not surprise anyone that the pursuit of a superseded standard should in fact amount to an exhaustion. The decision not to accept the fulfilment of the law, where and whenever that decision was made, was a serious fault. Viewed as part of the universal mechanism, such a decision tended to reverse a creative train of events, and for that reason it was necessary that all action arising from such a decision should inadvertently fail. The vast bodies of knowledge which were assembled as expressions of this failure were of course dead from the start. As dead bodies they simply had weight, and it was on account of this weight that the greatest purpose they served was laboursaving. Now it must be remembered that although labour is never necessary

35

since work accomplishes more even as a mere side-effect, it matters very much and is of grave importance how one goes about ceasing from labour and what one's reasons are for no longer labouring. In order to understand this more clearly, and because the very concept of labour tends to perplex by nature, we will define it in two different ways and will then compare it to the concept of work.

Labour defined in terms of its effect is an activity devoid of intrinsic meaning and mechanically stimulated. As such it can appear or not appear, it may or may not result in motion, and its purpose, which certainly can never be conceived, may be preconceived or else totally absent. Labour defined in the light of reason on the other hand is a human predicament and a problem specifically of the human mind when it has become divorced from the body, as only the human mind can. Interpreting this predicament intelligently and seeking not only a solution, but a creative solution to this problem, we are forced to participate in it and to identify with it as least to the slightest degree, only by way of experiment of course, so that we may demonstrate the cessation of labour, not as a reaction to it out of an observed knowledge of its effects, or as an attempt to remove it, or ourselves from it, on the basis of mere judgment, but in such a way that it becomes meaningful and therefore nonexistent. This last phrase of course contains the paradox, and there is no way around it but only the way through it by means of expression.

So that the divorce of mind and body be ameliorated, either the mind must be recreated, so that it may join the body, or the body must be reborn, so that it may unite with the mind. In either case the soul is established, and not merely an accident. It is not possible however for the sol to be established while the person labours. Again we might say that it either is a person or that it labours, but that both cannot be true at the same time, which is correct, but not very helpful. The imagination in the case of labour is not only not distinct, but it does not exist except merely so. This means that all images are spectral, which is to say uninvolved in reason, and luminous, which means that they are entirely set in darkness. The activity of labour is set off by such images, and the image strives through this activity to define itself and to become distinct. It is a fact that the presence of such images cannot be denied. How they came into being is of little interest to us here. Suffice it to say that the images exist and that their existence cannot be left undealt with. Knowledge of them however is not possible. Consequently they must either be radically transformed, which entails violence, or else they must be gradually exhausted, which requires the two essential qualities of care and toleration. Given these two qualities and a general spirit of devotion, the imagination is soon reconstituted. As soon as intolerance sets in however, the spectral image is allowed to express itself. This creates conditions of fragmented thought and of wicked emotion. Wickedness is an unsupported response of feeling. If carelessness sets in, the image is allowed to turn into an idol, and then it radiates an insane authority of its own and commences to exploit the mind, which in turn enslaves the body. And so it may occur that labour turns into an abuse of the flesh. A surplus of material inconsequence is amassed in the name of virtue or progress, and a surfeit of so-called laboursaving devices accumulates, both fashioned of matter and for the purpose of fashioning matter, which are in fact aggravations and frustrations of the labour process when the will runs amok or is bewildered, and when the intellect becomes promiscuous or obsessed.

Labour can be described as a process of purification and clarification which allows the human being to prepare for the eventual use of his senses and perhaps even for the employment of his brain. The human being which must labour may be described as the disinherited individual who has become subjected to his senses and whose brains have become a burden to him. Labour is in no relation whatsoever to work, since work involves love, and perhaps even a special love, which it makes. Labour is no more manual than it is mental, but it always arises where the manual and the mental are not differentiated. Labour is never physical of course. Only work can be physical, when it involves with equal intensity both the body and the mind. That is not labour which is to any degree at odds with time. If the individual's activity is based upon any appearance at all, such as the pursuit of fame or money, or such as popular agreement or admiration, he is neither working nor labouring. The only concept which really suits all activity other than work and labour is a waste of time.

Labour frees the will of the imperative of duty, and it liberates the intellect so that its spontaneity may be discovered and expressed. In labour one is always concerned with the difference between right and wrong and with the discernment between good and evil, but never with the goodness of the effect nor with the usefulness of what is right. What is more, labour is the only certain road for those whose will is castigated and whose intellect has become rigid to take them into the realm of voluntary limitation and eventual true freedom. People of this nature perceive only what their own efforts bring to their gaze, and then their perceptions are of course reflections of their own states and moods which are opined as existing outside of themselves. Their efforts during labour are those of the captivated narcissus and of the damsel in the presence of the unicorn. On one hand they struggle to free themselves from the fascination of their image which they mistake for an object, and on the other hand they attempt continually to turn their backs on the single principle which might guide them, which principle for that reason appears to them in the guise of a power both attractive and awful, and behind the mask of a strength at once regenerative and exhausting.

There is a way in which these people may be immediately helped. Let us presume that the reflections of their states and moods, which they mistake for objects, are actually turned into objects by the person who is aware of the true state of affairs. On the other hand let us postulate that the mask is made one with the strength which lies behind it, and that the guise is completely mixed with the power which it portrays. remembering that the mask, the guise and the mistaken reflections exist in response and in automatic response to human fault and weakness in the first place, we do not need to guess what will happen when reality is substituted for its imitation, its representation and its reproduction all in the name of truth and beauty. For we know that the fascination which accompanies the individual's appearance of his own image is an excellent antidote to the absolute stupor which would otherwise most certainly enter his dispossessed spirits, and we also know that the ambivalence of attraction and awe which coincides with the individual's presence of human power is a most beneficial contradiction to his vacillations between total forgetfulness of his lot and foolish anticipation of a premature fate; and furthermore that the ambiguity of new life and old life which concurs with the individual's apperception of human strength is a very valuable perplexity which prevents him on one side from rushing into action without foresight or hindsight, and forestalls on the other side his being engulfed and overwhelmed completely by the issue of his own heart. Once we understand the true purpose of the appearance, of the ambivalence and of the ambiguity, we need only to bring that purpose to perfection, and the individual will believe the reality whose substitute his own lack of faith brought about. We may sum up in this way, that he was helped to enter his strength through the door of his weakness; that he was brought to the recognition of his power by means of his feebleness and inconstancy, and that he came into the possession of real faith by breaking through the thin supports of his deafness and blindness.

*

The process which takes advantage of human lacks for the sake of real gain is that of art, and of live art. Extinct art recognized the lacks and created an illusory reality in detachment from those lacks. The illusory reality then allowed the individual to remove himself temporarily from his particular predicament of individuality, and encouraged him so to speak to take another look. Live art however creates the senses which are prerequisites for a true enjoyment of reality and at the same time it supplies that reality and establishes it automatically on the basis of humanity, which is the essence of being. Extinct art, in avoiding labour, creates a potential for it. Live art, which commences after the nature of labour has been fully comprehended, creates a capacity for work, and perhaps for that great work which is the making of a special love. A definition of live art is the human mastery of life and love in truth and in reality. Because of the nature of live art, which this definition of it demonstrates, as many definitions of it may be given as contain the essence of humanity in terms of human life. Another definition for example might be the creation of a oneness of nature and reality for the purpose of individual human life. It was necessary that a live science of mathematics was conceived prior to the conception of live art, even as it was necessary that live art was developed and perfected before a conception of a live mathematics could succeed. This should all be very obvious, because it springs directly from our definition of reality.

We go on now to define the various arts in terms of their specific purpose and with respect to the particular sense and capacities of mind which they involve and develop.

First it must be stated and stressed that no one art is more basic or fundamental, nor less successful or perfecting by definition in terms of personal human life, than any other art. And from now on, when we say art, we mean live art, and when we mean extinct art we will say so.

Music is the art which differentiates the brain. The human brain is the plenum. It contains all things and carries within it the capacity for the creation of all things. While it is undifferentiated, that capacity remains a capacity, and its content rests unexpressed. At such a time the human being does not act, but may only participate in certain activities, and all of these activities will be based upon reaction and resistance.

The first differentiation of the brain occurs as a function of duality. This means that action and passion become distinct and that they therefore imply each other intrinsically, that they complement each other extrinsically, and that they differ with reference to the shaping of appearances which is undertaken. In detail then, as has been treated by us elsewhere, action proceeds passionately, and passion entails an act. In greater detail, action makes use of the passions, and passion involves an application of our faculties. It is the nature of concrete sound to stimulate a duality of motive, and to bring about a unity of thought and emotion based upon common sense. Concrete sound is abstract sound which has been heard. Abstract sound is free of the matter which inhibits the sense of hearing, and it consists of nothing more than phonographic phenomena. Phonographic is the attribute which prepares seen substance for the purpose of the presence of substance as a whole. A phonographic phenomenon is an element of sound. A musical composition consists of such phonographic phenomena arranged according to a certain idea for the purpose of the realization of that idea. A musical composition is successful or it fails depending on whether that idea has been fully realized of not. An idea is fully realized when its meaning is both clear and plain. It is clear when it relates all the senses to each other and concentrates them in reasonable function. It is plain when it brings to bear the entire mind, and not just a part or an aspect of it, upon the body in the

41

creation of something significant. The successful musical composition of phonographic phenomena realizes a certain idea in such a way that it cannot be altered. No idea which has been realized can be altered of course, but this constancy of shape is the specific contribution and the unique emphasis and the foremost concern of musical realization.

It is important to keep in mind that no idea lends itself more readily to realization through one art than through another. There is no such thing as a musical idea. The realization of an idea may be generally analyzed as method, as manner and as technique. Under these three headings we may come to an understanding of how the various arts differ from each other. The synthesis which proceeds from the analysis is achieved through a study of the behaviour of each art, and this will yield an insight into each distinct art's practicum. Thereafter it remains to show how all the arts are similar, each in its own unique way coming to a conclusion as an end in itself and dependent only upon the principle of unfolding time.

The method of music is a contemporary elaboration of rhythm and rhyme. Rhythm is defined as structured repetition. Rhyme is defined as the colloquial concurrence of radical expression.

The manner of music refers to its change of apparent motivation. What we notice and understand as impulse and stimulus creates balance and harmony. Harmony is defined as the continuation of visible material.

The technique of music is a function of the performing will and of the creative intellect. They portray in unison and demonstrate relationships of a musical nature. We will discuss now what is meant by the nature of music.

The fantasy is the special faculty which creates musically. Perhaps we should inject here that creation in terms of nature entails destruction, which is liberation from structure. What the fantasy deals with must be at least free from structure, if not already involved in the creative process. It is a fantastic image

42

which is brought before the intellect and responded to by the will when the musically creative process begins. The image is fantastic when it spontaneously evokes an environment of sensibility, and it takes on that quality when the imagination and the fantasy interrelate. Images are then produced in immediate reality which are at once a means and an end in themselves. No response to such images is possible except by the will, and each and very response will be free of illusion and statically set in time. Since the nature of the responses is singular and quantitative they cannot be responded to again, and therefore any critical evaluation is forestalled. That is merely an incidental value however. Central to the issue is the purely quantitative response itself. It recreates itself automatically. Any resistance to it is immediately materially used up. The end of a process of recreation is always pleasure. When that process is automatic however, the pleasure is infinite.

A description of musical nature suggests its own perfect limitation. Of especial interest is the behaviour of what is called the musical line. It arises in response to the interpretative curiosity, and emerges as an image of as yet unlimited love. This image continues in existence only, of course, if it is right away limited and entirely so, and if it is not at all constrained. If it is constrained it collapses and retreats from view until such a time as is ruled again by patience and foresight. If it is not immediately and entirely limited, it is forced to take on structure, and that is approximately the same as when the fairy princess is harnessed to till the field. At once entirely limited, however, it is the shape of good beauty and an exceptional delight for the gourmet of the finest in art.

The nature of music begins where illusory nature leaves off. The very stuff of music is the fact. It is not possible to realize an idea musically without first describing it as fact. The essence of the fact is historical. Music permeates that essence with sound. A total permeation illustrates the historical process. If the existence of factual matter is accepted, we say that a musical treatment sets it to music. In this way the historical event is designated. In either case history is made and brought to the attention.

The most effective musical instrument is the human voice. It renders up human essence to human awareness, which means that it is immediately communicated. Any sound which the human voice produces is conspicuously musical. It is the tongue which manipulates that music and makes its production either creative or destructive. We speak or talk, we sing or chant, we weep or laugh, and in every case music may be the main source and the central aspect of what we do. This does not mean however that any of these must by definition contain music. They may also go on in reaction to music, in resistance to music, as an avoidance of, or an escape from music, and so on. To be as effective as their particular medium permits however, they must transport music.

Other musical instruments compare to the human voice much as the hand does to the soul they cannot be immediately assimilated by the body, but must first be studied and learned. If the human voice is studied and learned it becomes extinct. There are also such things as the tools of music, such as the sonata, the opera and the song, which as thought of as musical forms when they are extinct, but in the case of live music they may be employed as vessels and vehicles of pure musical substance, where the shape of the truth is proclaimed by means of the musical tool. The too has no meaning of course outside of this process of proclamation, and while the process goes on the tool is at best barely noticeable, but it does not contribute to the body of knowledge on its own account.

The trained voice is a dead voice. Its mere appearance lends itself to manipulation by sound in general. That sound is not created but construed and then set forth in a pattern of sorts, which pattern is then approximated in terms of preconceived notions and opinions which have been allowed to settle as custom. It is even possible to mistake custom for law, in which case the most expeditious corpses are set to walk about on the earth in lip-service to music, and the pleasure and enjoyment to be derived from them is summed up as the degree of fit between deceased sound and the essential model of decease, and those who delight in such a sort of perfection are welcome to it.

There is an immeasurable and unfathomable difference between that which is still alive and that which is alive again, and there are those who prefer what is entirely dead to that which is partially still alive. They are referred to as this generation, and the time of their reward has come. As they regard themselves in the light of reason for the first time, the monstrosity of their deeds comes home to them and they go out like a candle at the break of day, which is not to suggest that they have helped to light the night, because during the night they have refused to give solace and comfort, so that death might do his work more speedily and more thoroughly, and it is death who rewards them now in gratitude. It was necessary before they were removed that the new life should be established personally upon the earth, and since this has come about now, that has come to pass.

The essence of music is of universal appeal. What was defined as the colloquial concurrence of radical expression does not draw its attributes from a realm which is merely relative. Expression is radical when it demonstrates the very coming into being of what is human. At that level of knowledge the very basic law of expression itself is proclaimed, and that law is of universal and elementary import, as we implied in our philosophy. Colloquial on the other hand is not limited by an area of the earth's surface, but by that surface itself, and it describes the issue of primitive and archaic knowledge as it is uncritically perceived, as it is allowed to originate as an occurrence, and as it is upraised and appraised in terms of the mathematical system. Colloquial concurrence is the establishment of the autochthonous. Colloquial occurrence cannot be conceived because of the duality implicit in mere nature. Therefore every phenomenon which arises colloquially must be viewed simultaneously with its opposite, or else it is destroyed before it can become actual. Rhyme therefore can be described as a oneness of opposites and of those things which are opposite in reality.

Rhythm was defined as structured repetition. When repetition is destroyed there is vacillation, and then steadiness. destruction is part of the process of elaboration. To be contemporary means to be timed so as to continue only while the illusion of time lasts. The illusion of time is its passage. The elaboration of rhyme, contemporaneously with the elaboration of rhythm, achieves an ultimate agreement of time with space in terms of the human experience of natural beauty and personal truth on one hand and on the basis of reason as a medium on the other. There can be no doubt about the value of this method, since it achieves its end almost automatically, and needs only to be dealt with in awareness. It results in such music which is both naive and highly organized. By naive is meant an immediacy of recognition. Every musical composition of course will be a product of method, manner and technique at once, and not only of one or of two of these three. Classification of the product is according to whether technique is in pronouncement. Correspondingly one is given simply a musical composition if manner, method and technique are of equal importance, or else one has an opus in the case of technique, a piece of music in the case of manner, and a musical work in the case of method. Sub-categories may be invented if one of the three is appreciably absent.

Harmony was defined as the continuation of visible material. In the case of music this material is all the fluctuations of sound and silence, which may be abrupt or gradual. A degree of such fluctuation is called a note, and every note signifies a confrontation of sound and silence and gives an indication of the outcome of that confrontation. Harmony exists if the fluctuation between sound and silence is successfully limited, so that a noticeable texture of aural quality is present. Or we might say that harmony exists while notes mutually exclude each other in terms of strength and persistence. A single note cannot work harmony. Two notes exclude each other in terms of strength if their pitch differs sufficiently to allow a quantity of musical substance to be perceived, and they exclude each other in terms of persistence if their tonality differs sufficiently to allow a quantity of musical substance to be perceived. Tone is described as observed sound, while pitch is described as that quality of the sound for which one listens. The difference between listening and hearing is that listening involves the appearance of sound while hearing is the perception of sound in reality, which does or does not imply listening. Listening certainly does not imply hearing, although it may lead to it.

Music therefore must not necessarily be listened to in order to be heard. Listening is not a prerequisite of hearing. Hearing however is the necessary success of listening. Mere listening is an aberration of the senses.

Balance is described as evenness of quality in terms of energy, and in the case of music it refers to the quality of the sound. Descriptively again, the quality of sound may be observed, perceived or noticed, which renders it as tone, as pure sound, or as pitch. In terms of energy, tone is loud or soft, pure sound is audible or auditory, and pitch is high or low. Evenness of quality in terms of energy then means that no sound is understood as being loud or soft, high or low, audible or auditory, but as a carrier of the truth. Unevenness of quality diminishes the proficiency of the sound, and one becomes aware of isolated quality patterns.

The quality of the sound is transferred as physical stimulus or impulse. If the stimulus is noticed, the quality of the sound becomes apparent. If the stimulus is understood, the quality of the sound becomes flesh. Incarnate sound becomes visible as grace, as elegance, and as the art of the dance, which shall be discussed later. The noticed impulse renders the quality of the sound visible. The understood impulse makes it possible for the sound to be felt. Felt sound occurs as qualified vibrations which the brain interprets, so that emotions may be registered and so that thought may be produced for the support of those emotions.

Noticed sound stimulus is called noise. Noise cannot be heard, but it may be used in what is called an application of the ear. It forms an auditory backdrop then, against which the sense of hearing hears itself. This is a very special talent. It is the basis of what was once referred to as orison, or in the more distant past as listening to God speaking out of the whirlwind. Once noise has been accustomed in this manner, there is nothing left to offend the ear. The musical setting of hearing per se reveals reality in sound and such revelation forms the crux of the universal plethora of sound. Revelation in music must always be expressed or performed by the established human voice, and not by other instruments of music, since their rendering of sound cannot be whole. By the established human voice is meant the voice which is not any more trained or untrained, and which does not project sound or manipulate it, but which has become sound, and automatically demonstrates the order of things in audible terms.

It is music which illustrates most plainly the fivefold relationship between reality and nature. Music is most natural when it accompanies, and it is most real as melody. The accompanied melody sets forth the relation of logical simultaneity and demonstrates that relation in its greatest strength and permanence. The song, which is musical language, shows most readily how appearances are related to matter, which is a problem of singular complexity because it resides in the spontaneous. Musical language, or song, has no relation to speech. Speech is the concept of the word stated in fact, while song has no immediate connection to the word, but it is words felt and thought out on the basis of conscience. Speech is not an art, but it is the art, and when it is turned into an art it is called rhetoric, which compares to speech like the trained voice to the mature one.

The relation of subject and object becomes clear in music when the more customary sound accompanies the stranger one, and whenever an unfamiliar event seems to contradict the norm. The norm is of course always established during the composition, and it makes no sense either to attempt to adhere to it or to try to avoid it, since such behaviour can only satisfy us temporarily, because it springs from egocentricity. If the familiar and the strange complement each other, the developmental relation of subject and object makes possible optimum growth. The subject always seeks out what is most likely to fit, while the object searches for its opposite. When the fantasy is involved as in music, the subject and the object are able to align themselves for the purpose of wholeness without the instrumentality of any intermediary thing, and for that reason their confrontation can be perfectly peaceful.

The relation of truth and illusion is plain in music due to the shifts of tonality. A shift in tonality illustrates the impression of truth and distinguishes the twofold adaptability of that impression, on one occasion in terms of the developing subject, and on the other occasion direct and habitual. In terms of the developing subject the impression of the truth operates as parable, when it adapts itself freely to specific needs. The parable is truth through the medium of reason, and it delineates appearances in such a way that they become entirely transparent and reflectively acceptable as pure perception. Tonality is the sound mixture which involves appearances with feeling. A continued or sustained tonality deepens and complicates that involvement. The total experience of a perceived tonality in suspension is called a mode. While the suspension is supported and not divorced from meaning, the mode results in a thought complex which is a response to the emotional involvement of

49

appearances, and as the thought complex and the aroused feeling engage, knowledge is born, which entails a distribution of sense and the satisfaction of the certain desires. If the mode is avoided however, and if the tonality remains in flux, it registers quantitative changes of perception, and these quantitative changes are the shifts in tonality. Each one on its own account evokes fantastic imagination which is assimilated in the flesh. A shift from one mode to another provokes an entire image of fantasy, which must then first be translated perceptively before assimilation can take place.

If the impression of the truth is direct and habitual, the shift in tonality is adopted as a reasoned thing and then straightforwardly adapted. This means that it becomes a casual increase in strength evenly of body and mind, and that the soul rests more securely as a possessed thing. The effect of the musical phenomenon is then not pictured. Each shift in tonality invokes an amount of reason, and this is absorbed into the physical system. Again we are left finally with incarnate sound, and this increases the soundness of the flesh. The healing function of music becomes apparent here. It is not such a healing in this case which cures illness or sickness, since the healthy body is not capable of habitual truth in the first place, but the body must have been taken up into the physical system where it is beyond health and impaired health, but where a defect to the system, brought about by conscious experience or due to understood accident, leaves the body open to influence by the mind and exposes the mind to the influx of the body, such as in the case of rapture and ecstasy for instance. Healing then amounts to a reestablishment of mental and bodily position in union with the soul as physical growth takes place. The flesh, which is the viewed physical system, registers pleasure and stores it, while the brain, which is the head when it is viewed as part of the physical system, extracts from the flesh such matter which is about to be replaced directly prior to its replacement, and injects such substance into the body of knowledge which is re-membered as the apparatus of sensibility. We also say that the body of knowledge is sensitized, which implies its augmented capacity for sensation. The body of knowledge is the ordered sense organism which grows in size and dimension due to its systematic nourishment through physical experience, and this body of knowledge, which can grow infinitely, may be de-scribed in the appearances of the flesh. When music partakes in that description its manner is said to be exhibition.

The relation of natural phenomena and physical experience, which is the last to be discussed here, becomes plain in music due to just such an exhibition of the flesh. This takes us into the realm of the pornographic and of the obscene.

Once morality has completed its tasks, which it has, and the body and the mind are free of each other and established upon a common ground, which they are, there can be no more real disturbance when erotic energy is set loose. Erotic energy is not provoked, evoked or invoked then, but it is annexed. This annexation is achieved either by violence, or else by strategy. In the case of violence we speak of pornography when the nerve system is shocked, and in the case of strategy we are dealing with pornography when the nerve system is irritated. It must be emphasized here that the erotic does not intrinsically nor by definition have anything to do with sex, but that sex may certainly not be excluded. Sex and the erotic have become linked in popular fashion due to the fact that sex has always been the last factor which has had to be accepted before an erotic issue could be brought to the light. The association of sex and the erotic is sheer custom. Sexual energy is either pro-cured or construed, for the sake of marriage or during marriage, while the process of becoming one goes on, but once the mar-riage has succeeded, no matter who the persons involved were, sexual energy is a contrived thing and it is limited within the bounds of the erotic, since those who have become one do not continue to marry. The erotic may be referred to as the universal illusion of the flesh, but it cannot be defined, or perhaps we should say *and* it cannot be defined, for the same reason that incarnation cannot be defined, since it precludes definition. But we describe it as cosmic force and as an agent of human creation, perhaps the agent of human creation, in terms of which all creatures may be tamed and set free, and on account of which all things come to a ripe conclusion. In the case of violence we speak of obscenity when inhibitions are aroused or when extroversion of the senses themselves takes place, and in the case of strategy we speak of obscenity when the flesh is exhibited for the purpose of inhibition and when research goes on for the sake of knowledge and understanding of the physical per se. Inhibition, now that morality has been shed, is a valuable shield against abuse of the flesh, and it is like a protective covering for all the senses so that they are not liable to physical misuse. When the Jews were still free they practiced a cult of inhibition by circumcising male infants. Circumcision then became a concept for the state of sensibility of those whose senses had accepted and perceived the fulfilment of the law and who were therefore potentially exposed to the nonsense of all those who held fast to such customs and rites which had become defunct in the face of reality. Shame consequently is an inhibition, but it was and is not any more a sign of something, such as a sign of having transgressed wrongly or of having soiled oneself through illegitimate contact, but it is instead a symptom of a very unique process of knowledge, of growth through learning and teaching of physical matters in particular, when the shield is lifted so to speak in order to permit the rarity of the contact with the flesh, and it is a symptom of the contact with the flesh, and it is a symptom of a peculiar way of understanding, during submission to what is physically more powerful and in combination with the eager curiosity which may be aroused when confronted by the flesh which is holy. Similarly there is a pride, which is not vain at all, but good, and which is not based upon anything else except the perfecting conscience. Like shame, it is a symptom, but of manhood, and of the awareness of a power greater than which there is none. This power relates all the senses to each other, and to the intellect which guides them. It combines violence with authority and steeps strategy in the kind of wisdom which thrives on love. It is obscene therefore to demonstrate such pride because it cannot be brought under the control of consciousness, and such pride should be demonstrated, otherwise one's strength does not rise to its highest, and one's sense of purpose and perhaps of destiny cannot be enjoyed to the fullest. Obscenity which springs from violence gives evidence of a superabundance of strength which has been accumulated by force and intelligence. This overflowing of energy is by no means a waste, and certainly not a needless waste, but it may be compared to a bath in the liquid which makes the body invulnerable to injury and harm. Obscene is both the perception of such an occurrence and also the reason which instigates it, since that reason is not derived from something which is right of wrong, nor from what might be proper or improper, but it is based upon the pleasure of experience itself as it unfolds itself in pure thought and good will. The repulsion of the senses which sometimes introduces the obscene is terminal and may be neglected. The fascination with the obscene which sometimes strikes the human being may be interpreted as a mark of sense repression which urges the nourishment of that particular sense which has been appealed to, and the desire for sensation, which is distastefully obscene, shows a lack of cultivation of the environment. The obscene may even inspire horror. In that case the function of a particular sense is being improved. In combination with the grotesque and the perverse, the obscene tests our conscience directly, and if it is not pure we will suffer nausea and we will feel wretched. Then our conscience will be purged and the perverse element will be discarded.

In music obscenity is used as a function of chord and discord, and it is portrayed by means of sound texture. A chord is more than two simultaneous sounds. There is no such thing as a discord. To produce discord, simultaneous sounds are not enough, but there must be an element of sequence. Discord has nothing to do necessarily with unpleasantness to the ear. Noise must be produced, but whether or not the noise is distinguished depends entirely on the listener. The discord lies in the tension between sound and noise. This tension absolves. Obscenity is created when this tension achieves a response of intuition. The intuitive response may or may not be accepted. Obscenity exists in either case. Whether it works or not however depends upon whether the response is accepted and seen through or rejected and perhaps even negated. If it is accepted, the conscience is either purged or else uplifted, depending on whether it is pure or not. Absolution must not be an operation in order to be effective.

Pornography is an annexation of erotic energy by means of instinct and intellect. It is important that the brain is experimentally involved. All knowledge gained pornographically stems from an expansion of cosmic limitations. The cosmos is a view of change. It is limited only in terms of the body of senses, or in terms of the perceiving mind, which is the same. Pornographic knowledge then increases perceptibility, and the power of the senses as a whole. Cosmic limitations are expanded due to an extroversion of the perceiving mind, when the subject is not influenced but given over wholly, or, in the case of no subject, when substance is transferred as a description of mere essentials, and when appearances alone are rendered substantial. Saying the same in another way, cosmic limitations are expanded on account of the introversion of the sensuous body, when the object is accepted not piecemeal and progressively but at once and completely, or, in the case of no object, when substance is transferred as bare and unmitigated experience, and is inscribed into the flesh as an increase in physical size.

The study of pornography is called athletics, and the study of obscenity is called gymnastics. In both cases erotic energy is turned into physical strength. Extinct athletics neglects the mind for the sake of the body, and the body is only trained. Extinct gymnastics utilizes the body for the sake of the mind, and the mind is only trained. Live athletics and live gymnastics involve the mind and body simultaneously and in line with a certain principle of change which indicates or reflects the changing cosmos.

This brings us to the end of our introductory discussion of the art of music, and begins the discussion of the art of the dance.

*

The studies of athletics and gymnastics reveal a connection between the flesh and the brain which is physical in nature and accessible to mastery in reality. Physical energy is erotic energy which has been turned into strength. We keep in mind that strength is energy in action, while energy is potential strength. Now physical energy is immediately available to the human being once he has learned to master his body and his mind. The mastery of the body and of the mind entails their simultaneous growth. The flesh, which is the mind and the body in their physical state, creates its own mathematical counterpart which is appropriated by the brain. Because it is mathematical, which is how the brain as the plenum functions, this counterpart of the flesh, which is called the holy spirit, is taken up unchanged by the brain, and it is the brain which prepares it for work. Saying that the flesh creates the holy spirit is the same as to say that the holy spirit is poured out over all flesh. It is not true that the flesh makes the holy spirit. Making and creating should not become confused. But the creation of the holy spirit by the flesh is a phenomenon of our time, and it has not been this way since the beginning of time. It is also the phenomenon which brings all other phenomena to their just conclusion. We can see now how mathematics is a study of the workings of the holy spirit, and why it is true that the single failing which cannot help but lead to death is the insult to the holy spirit, since that is an outright injury of the brain and therefore destroys its capacity for bringing life to the flesh, whereupon the flesh dies.

The mathematical system can be viewed now as the flesh and the holy spirit linked by the brain. When we say brain we mean the human brain. The connection between the brain and the flesh is the human hand, and whatever the human hand does masterfully strengthens that connection. The connection between the brain and holy spirit is the human eye, and whatever the eye takes in masterfully strengthens that connection. The hand may be called the tool of the mathematical system, and the human eye is said to be the rule of the mathematical system. In the mathematical system all things are present absolutely, and in the concrete they make up what is called the kingdom. The human hand for example is the absolute tool, and as such it is present in the mathematical system. But simply as the human hand, granted that it is understood as the absolute tool, it is a physical thing in the kingdom. All physical things must be at least concrete, which means that they must have once been abstracted. Not all concrete things are physical however, since to become physical their position in the universal order, which is their catholic dimension, must be known. Not every human hand is a concrete thing therefore, since though it may be inwardly moved it need not a all be connected to the brain, not to speak of its being in itself the very connection between the brain and the flesh, and it may be moved mechanically, for which no brain is required, but only a nervous system.

*

56

The dance is the flesh at rest. Sound, which has become one with the flesh, instils meaning into a particular movement of the body, and then that meaning is not expressed, as perhaps in the gesture, nor is it demonstrated, as while walking for instance, but it is absorbed by the mind unexpressed and then felt and touched.

The dissolution of extinct flesh appears most commonly to the eye as a charming phenomenon, though this could never have been mentioned at the time. Charm constitutes an emotionally rewarding aspect of the dance and it may be discussed separately.

Once the illusion of rhythmic vitality has been discarded, as it must be if the flesh is to become more than a carrier of bodily functions, the concrete concentrate of perceived sense data takes its place and eventually becomes manifest as the original feature. Life which is temporarily featureless acquires, in direct conjunction with this art of the dance, the shape of its existence, and in such a way that there may be and can be no doubt about the result determined by its manifestation. A lack of complete feature, as on account of broken appearance, when the relation of body to mind was improperly established, is merely followed up with sufficient intention and the apparent connection is repaired.

The material by-product of the dance begins with the most inward renewal of our personal human essence and ends in the most terminal exemplification of myself.

The dance is from beginning to end oriented towards me. Whoever dances understands as much. This orientation is manifold in terms of experience and in terms of the dancer's environment it is simple and unique.

It is an artificial wish to distinguish between the dancer and the dance. It is readily conceded by the mind involved in the dance, or by the body that is taken up by the dance, that the central issue throughout the dance is my conquest of death. It is the one time in art that celebration is a prerequisite of the deed. Celebration alone, and that which is celebrated, namely always and again another manifestation of death as a tribute to life, these two may be distinguished, and usefully so.

———————